Elizabeth Ann Seton

Elizabeth Ann Seton
Wife, Mother, Sister, Saint

1774

A Biography for Young Readers
By Janet S. Wiley

Illustrations by Norbert Lenz

Nihil Obstat:
  Rev. Hilarion Kistner, O.F.M.
  Rev. John J. Jennings

Imprimi Potest:
  Rev. Andrew Fox, O.F.M.
  Provincial

Imprimatur:
  +Daniel E. Pilarczyk, V.G.
  Archdiocese of Cincinnati
  July 5, 1977

The *Nihil Obstat* and *Imprimatur* are a declaration that a book or
pamphlet is considered to be free from doctrinal or moral error. It
is not implied that those who have granted the *Nihil Obstat* and
Imprimatur agree with the contents, opinions, or statements expressed.

Illustrations by Norbert Lenz
Cover and book design by Michael Reynolds

SBN 0-912228-46-6

CONTENTS

Betty was a baby during the American Revolutionary War.

1. TWO BEGINNINGS

Church bells all over the land rang joyfully on September 14, 1975. On that day a new saint was named—Elizabeth Ann Seton. She became the first person born in the United States to be declared a saint by the Catholic Church.

Elizabeth Ann was born at the same time the United States was born. Her birthday was August 28, 1774, just a few months before the American Revolutionary War began on Lexington green in Massachusetts.

In her life Elizabeth showed many qualities that were an important part of the new nation—independence, courage, love of life, love of God, love of people, and hope—always hope.

She is famous for her work as a Catholic nun. But Elizabeth Ann Seton was not always a Catholic, and she was a wife and mother before she became a nun.

Her remarkable life began in the busy colonial port of New York. Her sister Mary was five when Elizabeth, nicknamed Betty, was born.

Her father, Richard Bayley, was a handsome young doctor. He loved his wife and two daughters very much. But when the Revolution began, he joined the British Army to serve his King as a hospital surgeon.

New York City, where Betty lived, was burned early in the war.

While he was away from home, the war swept into New York City. A gigantic fire destroyed 500 buildings and caused many people to flee. Mrs. Bayley and her children moved to Long Island.

The trouble proved too much for Betty's mother. She died the following May, 1777, when her third daughter, Catherine, was born.

Betty Bayley, at age two, was motherless.

From her schoolroom Betty watched hopefully for her father's carriage.

2. STEPMOTHER

Dr. Bayley soon brought home a new wife to be a mother for Mary, Betty and baby Catherine, whom they called Kitty.

Betty's new mother took good care of her three stepdaughters. She taught prayers to the older girls.

But a very sad thing happened. Baby Kitty died. When a grown-up asked Betty why she was not crying for her sister, Betty said, "Kitty is gone up to heaven. I wish I could go, too, with Mama." Betty remembered her own mother and missed her very much.

Betty was proud that her father was the first doctor in New York City to drive a carriage on his calls. Other doctors walked or rode horseback. Still, she wished that he would not always be so busy.

Often she would watch out the window at school for

his carriage to go by in the street. Once she jumped up from her desk and ran out to him as he passed.

A new baby was born at the Bayley house every year. Mrs. Bayley could not give much time to Mary and Betty.

Finally when Betty was eight, she and her sister Mary were sent to live on their Uncle William's farm in New Rochelle, 17 miles from New York.

Here for city-born Betty a new world opened up—the world of nature. How she loved to run happily through fields of daisies or lie quietly on the moss under a tree! Everything in God's wonderful world delighted her. Rocks, stars, sheep, clouds, ice—all were his miracles.

Since Uncle William's farm bordered the seashore, Betty, Mary and their cousins played on the beach. They gathered shells and skipped barefoot at the water's edge.

One day the children found a bird's nest with eggs in it. Just to see what would happen, one of the girls threw the eggs to the ground. Inside the smashed eggs were tiny young birds with beating hearts. Betty knelt beside the wee bits of life and tenderly placed them on a leaf. Betty was crying. She felt sure that the mother bird would return and make everything right.

To the little girl who longed for a mother's love, it seemed that the power of such love could do anything.

Playing the piano was fun.

3. GROWING UP

Many of Betty's relatives lived on estates near Uncle William's farm. The kindly gentleman welcomed housefuls of cousins, aunts and uncles.

One of Betty's favorites was Miss Molly B., an elderly aunt who had lived most of her life in France. During their happy afternoons together, Miss Molly B. taught Betty to speak and read French. All her life Betty liked to say her prayers in French.

Betty and Miss Molly B. both loved the Bible and never tired of reading it together. Music was another joy to Betty, and she learned to play many songs on the piano.

In her early teens Betty returned to her father's house in New York for two years. She found the city, the capital of the new nation, bustling with excitement. George Washington was to be inaugurated the first President of the United States!

There were many things to do at her uncle's house.

Dr. Bayley had promised to take Betty, and she could hardly wait for the great day to arrive. She was especially anxious to see the President's splendid inauguration suit. It was made completely from materials produced in the United States. Not a button or a buckle had come across the ocean from another country.

Like other girls of wealthy families, Betty spent her days sewing, writing letters, practicing music, taking walks, riding horseback and going to teas. But reading was Betty's favorite pastime. She loved to meet new people, new places and new ideas in the many books in her father's and her uncle's libraries.

When she was 19,
Betty married William Seton.

4. PRINCE CHARMING

In the evenings, with black curls piled high on her head, Betty would often go with her friends to a play, a musical program or a dance. Many young men wanted this gay, pretty girl for a partner.

Then one evening Betty's Prince Charming appeared. He was the rich and handsome William Seton. Dozens of young girls peeked at him over their fans, but it was little Betty Bayley who won his heart.

Will had just come home from Europe. He could describe for Betty all the exciting places she had read about.

He too loved music and played the violin for her. In fact, his violin had been made in Italy by Stradivarius, the world's most famous violin maker. It was the first

Stradivarius violin in the United States.

Will's parents, who had 13 children of their own, welcomed Betty warmly.

Life looked bright indeed for Betty and Will when they were married in 1794. Betty, at age 19, had a home to call her own at last. She could hardly believe that God had been so good to her.

The home that Will brought Betty to was on Wall Street. At that time Wall Street was a boulevard lined with trees and elegant mansions. Alexander Hamilton, the first Secretary of the Treasury of the United States, was a neighbor of the Setons.

What fun the young couple had furnishing their new home! Will had joined his father in his merchant business.

The company named one of its graceful clipper ships
<u>Elizabeth Seton</u>, in honor of the newest member of the Seton
family. Betty had her choice of the best American or
imported tables, chairs, beds, dishes, linens and rugs. She
even had servants to help her.

A baby, Ann, born the next year, made Betty and Will's
joy complete. Now they liked best to stay home by a
crackling fire and enjoy their good life together.

But sometimes the Setons still went to parties and balls.
Will was one of four hosts at a party to celebrate President
George Washington's 65th birthday. Elegant ladies and
gentlemen came to the capital from all over the new nation,
to honor their first President. They found sparkling Betty
Seton there to greet them.

**Many people were coming to live in the United States. Dr. Bayley,
Betty's father, helped to take care of them if they were sick.**

5. THE OTHER NEW YORK

Not all of New York was a place of beauty and gay times. There were big problems in the fast-growing city.

Sickness raged every year, killing thousands of people. Malaria, croup and yellow fever were dread diseases.

The city set up a board of health to tackle the problem. The man chosen to be the first Health Officer of the City of New York was Dr. Richard Bayley, Betty's father.

Dr. Bayley was a brilliant man. He knew that the smelly garbage ditches in the streets and the muggy swamps around the city were causing much of the trouble. He tried to show city and state leaders that New York must be cleaned up if epidemics were to be stopped.

Another problem was that immigrants, people who came from other countries to live in America, often brought sickness with them.

One of Dr. Bayley's jobs was to examine and treat the immigrants, who were pouring into New York by the boatload. He set up a medical station on Staten Island in New York harbor to help prevent the spread of disease to the city.

Dr. Bayley's greatest comfort during this very busy time was visiting Betty and Will. Betty and her father grew closer to each other than they ever had been before.

If telephones had been invented, they surely would have talked together every day. As it was, Betty and her father sent letters back and forth with their houseboys, or by post when he traveled out of town.

Betty could not live a carefree life with so much misery all around her. So she and some of her generous friends formed the "Widows' Society."

They sewed clothing and took it to people in need. They raised money to help the poor. Betty became treasurer of the group.

The Setons bought a summer home on Long Island because they did not want to stay in the city when sickness was at its worst. Two more babies were born to them, William and Richard.

Yellow fever struck both Will Seton and baby William, but they got well. While nursing them, Betty often turned to God in prayer. She wrote to a friend, "I have become a looker-up."

Betty would have need to be a "looker-up" in the years that lay ahead.

Ships owned by the Setons brought wonderful things from all over the world.

6. A BIG FAMILY

When Grandfather Seton, Will's father, fell on the ice one winter day, the family did not worry very much. He went to bed to rest and recover.

But Grandfather's injuries did not heal quickly. He grew weaker and became ill. Quite suddenly, Grandfather was gone.

All of a sudden, life had changed for Betty and Will.

Since Will was the oldest Seton son, he and Betty became father and mother to the seven youngest Seton children. Now Betty had 10 children to care for.

Eighteen-year-old Rebecca Seton, Will's sister, was a great help to Betty. Together they did the daily chores, sewed, tended the babies and ran a little school for the younger children. Betty and Rebecca grew to love each other dearly.

The older Seton boys and girls went to boarding schools in Connecticut and New Jersey. Sometimes they brought home friends for the holidays. Even with the family servant, Mammy Huler, to help, these were busy times for Betty and Rebecca.

New responsibilities were also heaped upon Will. When his father died, Will became head of the Seton merchant fleet. The new duties and decisions were hard for the young man. Often after the children went to bed, Betty would sit for hours by candlelight, helping Will with his account books.

Although they worked hard, the business began to fail.

Pirates captured many of the Seton ships loaded with valuable cargo. Storms wrecked other ships.

When a Seton ship sailed into New York harbor, Betty would hurry to the dock to greet it. But as the months wore on, fewer and fewer Seton ships arrived. The Setons had to sell their summer home and some of their furniture to pay their debts.

Will became discouraged. Betty tried to show him that they still had many blessings. She was sure that brighter days lay ahead. He lovingly called his tiny wife "my old knot of oak."

Betty's real worry was William himself. As long as she had known him, he had always coughed more than most people. Now he was coughing harder and more often than ever.

7. PEACEFUL MOMENTS

With all of her troubles, Betty still found many joys in life.

Another daughter was born, and Betty delighted in the child's sweetness. Baby Catherine, named for Betty's mother and sister, made everyone smile at her christening. She laughed out loud when the cold water touched her head.

Betty and her children spent a happy summer with Dr. Bayley on Staten Island. Will's young brothers and sisters were visiting other relatives, and Betty could enjoy a much-needed rest. Will sailed over the bay to be with his family on weekends. Although Dr. Bayley was busy during the day with the immigrants at the Staten Island hospital, he was a loving grandfather after working hours.

Here in the open air of the country Betty could discover again with her children the beauty of nature. A feeling of great peace would come over her as she watched a glorious sunset.

Back in the city she found strength and comfort in going to Trinity Episcopal Church. She decided that whatever happened to her, she would dedicate her life to God. She would put herself in his hands.

She was happiest on Sacrament Sunday, when bread and wine were distributed to the congregation. Rebecca shared Betty's great faith in God. Betty called Rebecca her "Soul's Sister."

Reverend Henry Hobart, the minister at Trinity Church, gave fine sermons that helped Betty and Rebecca grow in their love of God. Reverend Hobart became their good friend.

With his encouragement, the Widows' Society grew. Sometimes Betty and her friends were called the "Protestant Sisters of Charity." They gathered goods from wealthy friends and gave them to needy families. Even though her own troubles were growing, Betty never forgot the suffering poor of New York.

Betty loved to watch her children play.

Betty was sad when her father died.

8. GOODBYE, GOODBYE

The new century did not bring a change of fortune to Betty and Will.

In fact, just before Christmas in 1800, Will was forced to admit that his business was wiped out. He declared bankruptcy and sold all the ships and goods of the merchant company.

The Setons moved to a less expensive house near a park called the Battery. From here they had a splendid view of the ocean, where Seton ships sailed no more. Will vowed that he would repay every debt he owed. He began looking for some way to make a new start. But his health was poor.

It was also at this time that working with sick immigrants finally caught up with Dr. Bayley. He caught the dreaded yellow fever. Fearlessly and tenderly Betty and her sister Mary cared for their father. Within a week, Dr. Bayley died.

Since he had died of yellow fever—or the plague—the city officials would not allow his coffin to pass through the city streets. Wishing to have her father and mother buried together, Betty hit upon the idea of using her father's own boat to carry the coffin up the river to a spot near the cemetery. Only a few relatives and friends were brave enough to attend the burial of this courageous, generous man.

A fifth child, Rebecca, was born to Betty and Will. The new baby was sick much of the time. Mammy Huler, the faithful Seton servant, died. Betty worked day and night in a brave effort to keep the household and the daily lessons running smoothly. But soon it became clear that Will was dying of tuberculosis.

At last Betty and Will decided to go to Italy, in the hope that sunny weather would help him. Will had good friends in Italy. He had spent many happy boyhood days there.

They sold their home, their furniture, pictures, silver—

almost everything. Reverend Hobart kept Betty's piano for her and a few other treasures. Reverend Hobart said a strange thing to Betty: "Do not let the splendid religious worship in Italy draw your heart away from the simple worship of Trinity Church."

Finally the day came to sail. They took their eight-year-old daughter Ann with them, but the other children were too little for the long, dangerous ocean voyage.

Rebecca Seton, whom Betty loved and trusted above all others, took charge of the children. Even so, Betty's heart was breaking as she waved goodbye to her little ones from the deck of the ship. She did not know if she would ever see them again.

In the carefree days before their wedding, Will had gaily promised to take Betty to Europe someday. Now, at age 29, Betty was indeed sailing to, Europe with Will. But it was not as they had planned.

Antonio Filicchi sent help to Betty, Will and Ann.

9. STORM AND TROUBLE

During the voyage Ann had whooping cough, but Will seemed stronger in the ocean air. With joy in their hearts, mother, father and daughter saw the pleasant green hills of Italy rise before them.

When the gangplank was lowered, Will started down with arms outstretched to greet his friend Antonio Filicchi, who had come to meet the ship.

"Don't touch!" a sailor commanded rudely.

Then the dreadful news was told. Because of his coughing, which was feared to be the plague, Will would have to go to the nearby immigrant station for a time. The family would not be allowed to land. Just like the sick immigrants in New York, they were now sick immigrants in a foreign land.

Betty expected to see a hospital like her father's

The Setons had a hard time in Italy.

hospital in New York, one which cared for the patients.

But the family was rowed out to a tall stone building built like a prison. They were locked in a cell on the second floor.

There was nothing in the cell. No heat, no bed, no chair—nothing. Betty had brought a few books and a little clothing from the ship. A mattress was brought in for Will to lie on. Then a violent storm blew up, and wind whistled through every crack in the cold stone walls. This is the hour of trial, thought Betty.

The "hour of trial" lasted one month.

They all lived through it by the grace of God and the goodness of Antonio Filicchi.

Antonio sent food, charcoal, beds, blankets, curtains and toys. But most important, he sent an old family servant, Luigi.

Luigi lived in the cell next to the Setons'. He cooked, tended the fire, went for medicine and ran other errands. One day he even brought flowers.

Sometimes Betty and her daughter Ann skipped rope to keep warm.

The family passed the time mostly by reading and praying. They dreamed of heaven, where the whole family would be together again.

Smoke from the fire, the dampness and the chilling wind nearly killed Will. He seldom got out of bed. He coughed constantly and he ate little. Once a doctor came to look at Will and said, "You do not need me. You need a minister."

On December 19 the prisoners were freed and Will was carried ashore.

He lived long enough to celebrate Christmas with Betty and Ann. Then Will's suffering ended.

When Will died, Betty turned to God for help.

10. GOOD FRIENDS

The Filicchis were true friends to Betty and her daughter. To take her mind off her sorrow, they took Betty to see some of Italy's most beautiful churches and museums.

Betty had never seen such magnificent churches. She loved them. When Antonio offered to take her to a Protestant church one Sunday morning, Betty said, "No, thank you. I would like to go to a Mass with you."

Betty liked the idea that Catholics had daily Mass and could receive Communion any day. She also welcomed the idea of Mary being a Mother to everyone.

The very day that their ship was to sail for America, Ann became ill with scarlet fever. Betty caught it, too. Antonio and his wife nursed them slowly back to health. Betty came to see that Catholics, as well as Protestants, could show unselfish love for others.

When again the time came to leave, Betty did not know in which Church she belonged. She also wondered what life would be like without Will. But Philippo, Antonio's brother, comforted her: "My little sister, God takes care of little birds and makes the lilies grow. I tell you he will take care of you."

11. THE CHOICE

Four healthy, happy children—William, Richard, Catherine and baby Rebecca—were waiting on the dock in New York to greet their mother and sister. How happy Betty was to hug her little ones again!

But when she looked up at the group of relatives, she asked, "Where is Rebecca?" Then she learned that her "Soul's Sister" was near death. It seemed as if Rebecca had stayed alive just waiting for Betty's return.

When Rebecca Seton died, Betty had nobody to talk to about her religious ideas. She tried to talk to Reverend Henry Hobart, but he was very stern with her. He said, "I warned you. Have nothing to do with Catholics. They will try to poison you with their lies. If you become a Catholic, I will have nothing more to do with you." Betty shivered at the cold warning.

From Antonio she received this advice: "Pray! Study both religions to find the truth. Whatever you do, I will be your friend forever." Betty was warmed by his kind promise.

Each man wanted what he thought was best for Betty.

Betty wrote letters to priests in Boston and Baltimore telling of her confusion. They answered her questions kindly. She read many books about religion.

She said a prayer that she had learned by a famous poet:
> "If I am right, O teach my heart
> Still in the right to stay.
> If I am wrong, thy grace impart
> To find the better way."

Finally Betty made up her mind. One morning she walked up Barclay Street to St. Peter's, the only Catholic Church in New York City, and announced to Father O'Brien, "I want to become a Catholic."

The simple words shattered Betty's old life.

Most of her relatives and friends felt as Reverend Hobart did. They did not want Betty or her children in their homes any more.

A few people were faithful to Betty all their lives, including her sister Mary. Two little Seton girls, Cecelia and Harriet, whom Betty had mothered, never stopped loving her. In fact, little Cecelia ran away from her sister's house once to go and live with Betty.

At home in New York, Betty joined the Catholic Church.

But the Seton doors—and many others in New York—
were closed to Betty when she became a Catholic.

Most of the Catholic people in New York were poor
immigrants. They were often dirty. The men spit. They spoke
loudly and shoved each other. Their homes were shabby.
Most had not gone to school. But Betty looked into their
hearts and saw the same deep faith that she had seen in Italy.

Her father, Dr. Bayley, had died caring for immigrants.
Betty had often carried food and clothing to them. She was
not ashamed to kneel and pray with them now.

With her children Betty sailed to Baltimore to teach school.

12. A NEW START

How was Betty going to provide a home, food, clothing and education for her five children?

She tried teaching in a little school. But Protestant parents did not want a Catholic teacher for their children. So the school failed.

She tried taking in children to live with her while they were attending a nearby school. But the children were rude and disobedient because she was a Catholic. So that idea failed.

Antonio suggested that she and her children come to Italy to live. There her life would be much easier. The idea was tempting. But Betty was an American. She felt that no matter how hard it was, her duty lay in America. So here she stayed.

Then Antonio said he would pay for the education of

her sons. Even with this generous help, it was impossible for Betty to make ends meet in New York.

A priest in Baltimore, Maryland, learned of her difficulty. He said, "We have many Catholic families in Maryland. We need schools. Will you come here to teach?"

Betty agreed. She was happy to be needed.

So one bright morning in June, 1808, a little boat sailed out of New York harbor bound for Baltimore. Aboard was Betty Seton with her children, about to begin the greatest adventure of her life.

13. BRIDE OF CHRIST

Betty was welcomed in Baltimore with all the warmth of a homecoming, although she had never been there before. Many neighbors came to greet the new schoolmistress from New York.

Her red brick schoolhouse soon held 10 young pupils. The children lived at the school. Betty was happy and busy caring for them. Religious teaching and prayer were an important part of every day.

Two young girls came to help Betty in her work. Many more students wanted to come. It became clear that a bigger school was needed.

At the same time Betty's love for God grew deeper and deeper. She dreamed of becoming a nun. But her first duty was to her children. How could a mother of five children become a nun? She never would give up the care of her children.

Bishop John Carroll of Baltimore saw that Elizabeth Seton was a rare treasure. She had deep religious faith, courage, kindness, intelligence—qualities which the head of a new religious community would need. So he gave Betty special permission to become a nun. Her three daughters would stay with her. Her boys were already away at boarding school most of the time.

With great joy Betty became a "Bride of Christ." She was now known as Mother Seton. Indeed, she was to become the mother of many daughters.

Her helpers decided to wear black dresses like the one Mother Seton had been wearing since Will died. A white cap completed their outfit or habit.

Mother Seton and her helpers called themselves the Sisters of Charity. It was the first native American sisterhood.

Mother Seton wrote to her friend Antonio Filicchi for money to build a bigger school. But before he could answer, a wealthy man from Baltimore offered $10,000 for the purpose.

The generous man purchased farmland near the town of Emmitsburg, Maryland, 50 miles from Baltimore. Nearby was a boys' school, Mount St. Mary's. Here, in this ideal spot, Mother Seton would build her school.

Betty became a sister and began the Sisters of Charity.
She was called "Mother Seton."

Joyfully Mother Seton traveled to Emmitsburg to set up a bigger school.

14. EMMITSBURG

True pioneers, Mother Seton and her band loaded their belongings into a covered wagon and set out. The driver was a boy from Emmitsburg who had come for them.

The Sisters of Charity owned three mattresses, two lanterns, chairs, pots and pans, candles, soap, linens, blankets, dried meat, vegetables, tea leaves and three loaves of bread. Mother Seton also brought some religious paintings and statues and Will's Stradivarius violin.

The wagon bumped along the two ruts that served as a road. The Sisters sang and told stories as they walked behind it. They lifted their skirts and waded barefoot through streams.

The huge sky arched overhead and Mother Seton's heart swelled with love for God's creation. Life was a glorious adventure.

Life was hard, but beautiful, at St. Joseph's.

People in towns stared in amazement as the Sisters passed. A group of women traveling through the wilderness was a strange sight indeed!

After three days mountain peaks rose up ahead of the travelers. In a valley lay Emmitsburg. They had arrived.

A log cabin was the Sisters' first home. That night, weary but happy, the pioneer women spread their mattresses on the dirt floor and slept.

Soon a larger stone house with four rooms was ready and school began. Children from the countryside came, eager to learn. Both black and white children attended the school. Most of them were poor. So Mother Seton saved apples and milk from her cupboard for them. The Sisters also visited sick people in Emmitsburg and the surrounding countryside.

The first winter was a hard one. Snow blew in through chinks in the windows. The Sisters washed clothes in a creek and boiled carrot tops to make a drink they called "carrot coffee."

In the spring they planted a garden. Later they bought a few cows, chickens and pigs. A horse was given to them, and Mother Seton and the other Sisters loved to take rides in the country.

The fame of Mother Seton and her Sisters of Charity spread quickly. Many young girls wanted to join Mother Seton in her work for God. Many families wanted to send their daughters to her for education. A still larger house and school was completed. The year was 1810, just two years after Betty Seton had left New York for Baltimore.

Sisters of Charity spread love wherever they went.

15. WIDENING CIRCLES

Mother Seton was a good teacher. Girls who came to her school, St. Joseph's, learned reading, writing, spelling, grammar, geography, history, arithmetic, religion, music, needlework and languages. They were trained to become Christian adults. Mother Seton's school was the first Catholic parochial school in the United States.

When Mother Seton had to punish a child, she often made the girl kneel before the altar in the chapel for a while. Mother Seton was quick to praise good work and she gave little religious pictures as prizes. She sent short notes to students to praise or encourage them. When a frightened new student alighted from her carriage at the school door, she would find herself being greeted and hugged by the school director.

Many of Mother Seton's pupils wrote to her after they left school. They asked for advice or shared their joys. She was never too busy to answer every letter.

At the same time Mother Seton gently but firmly trained the novices—young girls who wished to join the Sisters of Charity. She copied religious books from French into English for them to study.

Her experience with the Seton merchant company helped her keep the account books for the school and the Sisterhood. The school did well under her care.

Her day began at 5:00 and ended only after the girls were in bed. But they were days of joyful service to God.

Her sister Mary made the long trip from New York to visit her. So did a few other faithful friends from her younger days. As years went by, even the Setons began to feel proud of her and wrote her letters. She answered them with love, as if no unkind thing had ever happened.

Sorrow was never far from Mother Seton's heart. One by one, loved ones died and were buried in the grove of trees near her school.

Harriet and Cecelia Seton, Will's sisters, were the first ones to be buried in the cemetery. They had become Catholics and had joined Mother Seton in Maryland. Ann and Rebecca, her oldest child and her youngest, died of tuberculosis, like their father.

Each death was a great loss to Mother Seton. But she had learned long ago not to hold on too tightly to anything in this world. Her only wish was to please God. Once she said, "Can we expect to go to heaven for nothing?"

A wonderful day came when the Bishop of Philadelphia asked Mother Seton to send three Sisters to his city to open an orphanage. She did so, and many homeless children found a home with the good Sisters.

Next, three Sisters were called to New York to set up another orphanage. Mother Seton was happy to send Sisters to her own city, New York.

A pebble dropped into a pond sends out circles of ripples that grow wider and wider. The goodness of Mother Seton was spreading throughout the United States through her daughters, the Sisters of Charity.

Mother Seton's white house still stands in Emmitsburg.

16. AN AMERICAN SAINT

"Open the window so that I can hear the children," Mother Seton said. One of the Sisters opened the window. A smile came to Mother Seton's lips. Even as she lay dying of tuberculosis, the sound of the happy voices gave her joy.

A sister spoke a prayer to the Virgin Mary in French. Then quietly and peacefully, on January 4, 1821, Mother Seton died. She was only 46.

One hundred-fifty-four years later, in 1975, the Catholic Church named Mother Seton a saint. Episcopalians also rejoiced.

A saint is a person who pleases God. A saint can be a farmer, a housewife, a king, a poet, a nun, a child.

In war, some soldiers receive medals for bravery. But many brave soldiers never receive medals.

In sports, the very best players are named to a Hall of

Fame. But many fine players are never named to a Hall of Fame.

So it is with saints. The most holy servants of God are canonized, or officially named as saints. The Catholic Church teaches that they have gone to their reward in heaven. But many saints are in heaven who were never canonized on earth.

Mother Seton was named Saint Elizabeth Ann Seton after years of study and prayer by wise and good men and women.

Only in America was it likely to happen. A Catholic saint raised as an Episcopalian; a society belle who became a pioneer; a nun who was also a mother. Such a glorious mixture was Saint Elizabeth Ann Seton, the Catholic Church's treasure and America's pride.